The DRAGON

and

RAT TALE

COLORING BOOK

Donnabelle Pineda

author**HOUSE**

AuthorHouse™
1663 Liberty Drive
Bloomington, IN 47403
www.authorhouse.com
Phone: 833-262-8899

Published by AuthorHouse 01/30/2021

ISBN: 978-1-6655-0790-5 (sc)
ISBN: 978-1-6655-0791-2 (e)

This coloring book belongs to:

_____

Use this page to draw or write a story about the picture on next page.

Help Dragon get to Rat and bring her back to the castle.

Use this page to talk about your day.

Dragon and Rat Characters

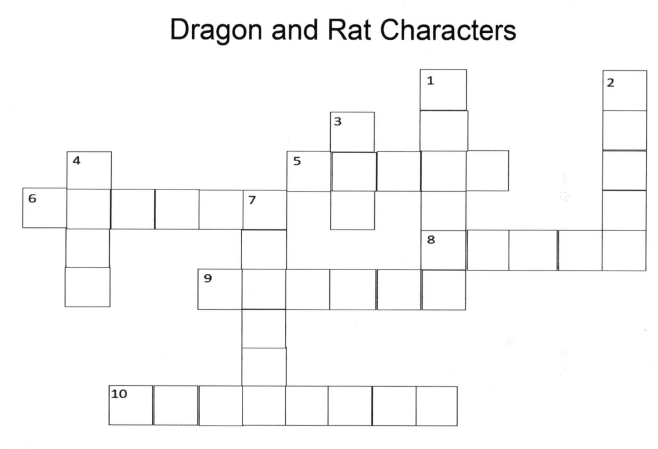

DOWN

1. Son of king and queen,
2. Mother of prince or princess.
3. Creature that loves cheese.
4. Father of prince or princess.
7. Humongous fiery winged monster.

ACROSS

5, Mystical powers
6. Person who has magical powers
8. Hat that royalties wear on their head.
9. The place where kings and queens live.
10. Daughter of king and queen.

10

Use this page to draw anything you want.

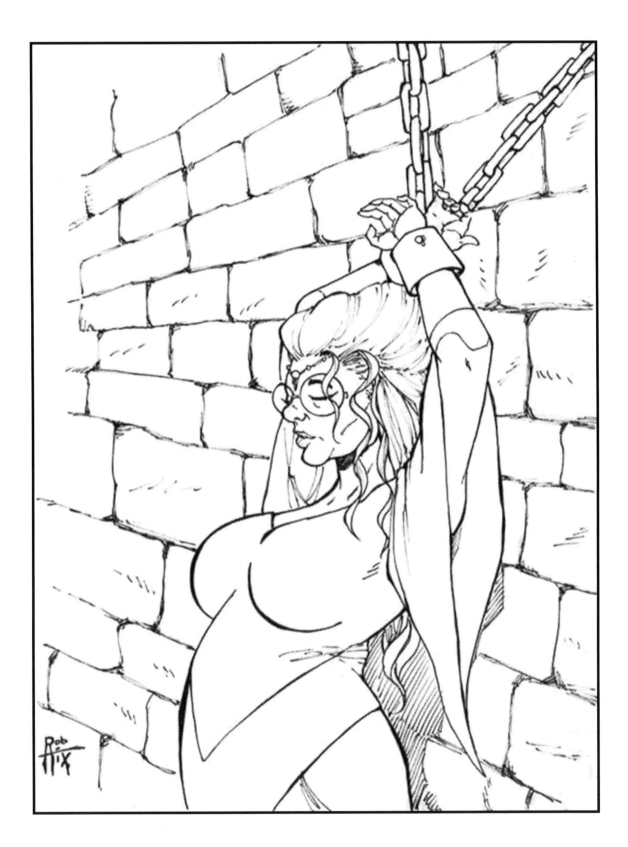

Connect the dots

13

Use this page to draw your favorite character in this this book and post on The Dragon and Rat Tale FaceBook page. You can also say why it is your favorite character.

Matching Lists With Images

rat

star

drum

cake

king

triangle

watch

bell

butterfly

castle

tree

square

Jayla's Bearded Dragon

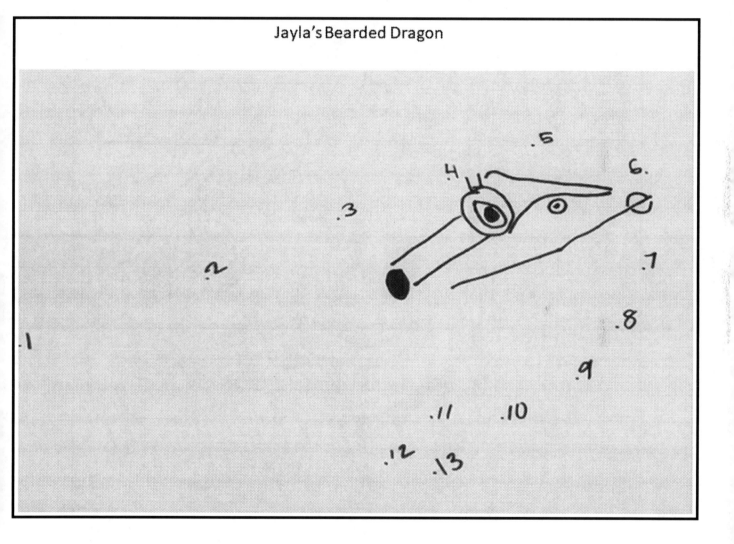

Word Search

```
M U Y M F R I E N D
P O Y H A I Y P U Z
R F T K B G K Y N W
I Q J H P R I N C E
N Z U P E K N C X F
C L B E Y R G S A L
E O C R E A T U R E
S V Z O D N N B R L
S E D R A G O N A L
C H I V A L R Y T W
```

CREATURE   PRINCESS   CHIVALRY   MOTHER
DRAGON   PRINCE   QUEEN   MAGIC
FRIEND   KING   LOVE   RAT

Match words with pictures

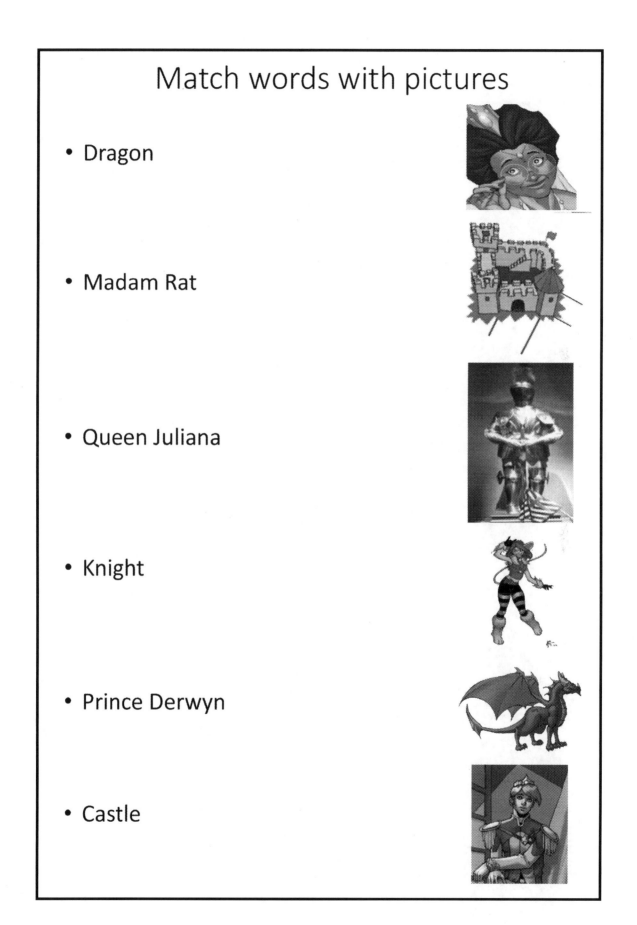

- Dragon

- Madam Rat

- Queen Juliana

- Knight

- Prince Derwyn

- Castle

2018

Matching Lists With Images

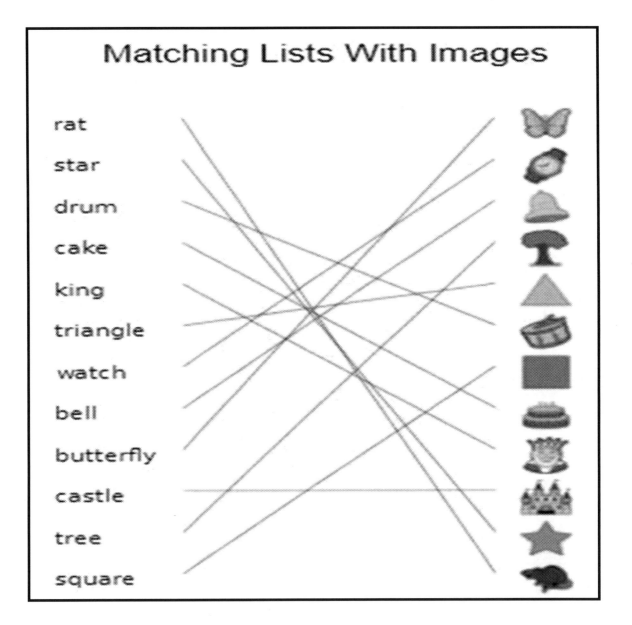

rat

star

drum

cake

king

triangle

watch

bell

butterfly

castle

tree

square

Dragon and Rat Characters

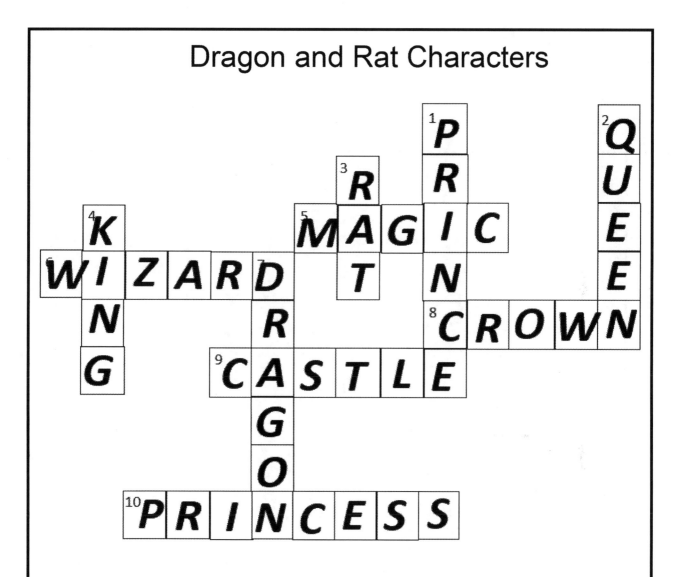

DOWN

1. Son of king and queen,
2. Mother of prince or princess.
3. Creature that loves cheese.
4. Father of prince or princess.
7. Humongous fiery winged monster.

ACROSS

5, Mystical powers
6. Person who has magical powers
8. Hat that royalties wear on their head.
9. The place where kings and queens live.
10. Daughter of king and queen.

Word Search

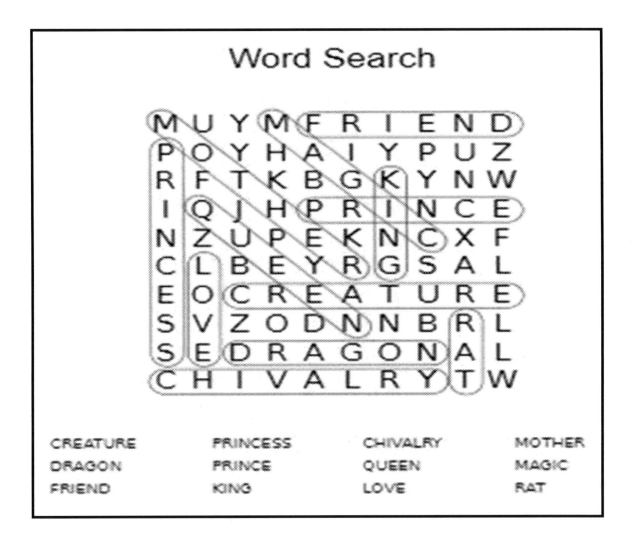

M	U	Y	M	F	R	I	E	N	D
P	O	Y	H	A	I	Y	P	U	Z
R	F	T	K	B	G	K	Y	N	W
I	Q	J	H	P	R	I	N	C	E
N	Z	U	P	E	K	N	C	X	F
C	L	B	E	Y	R	G	S	A	L
E	O	C	R	E	A	T	U	R	E
S	V	Z	O	D	N	N	B	R	L
S	E	D	R	A	G	O	N	A	L
C	H	I	V	A	L	R	Y	T	W

CREATURE	PRINCESS	CHIVALRY	MOTHER
DRAGON	PRINCE	QUEEN	MAGIC
FRIEND	KING	LOVE	RAT

32

Answers to Match words with pictures

- Dragon

- Queen Juliana

- Madam Rat

- Knight

- Prince Derwyn

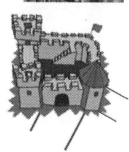

- Castle

Thank you to my granddaughter Jayla for helping me with ideas on moving forward with The Dragon and Rat Tale coloring book version. This is another activity she can do with her baby sister Ofa and baby brothers.

References:
https://www.education.com/

Facebook page:
https://www.facebook.com/pages/category/Book/The-Dragon-and-Rat-Tale-602616643492665/

Instagram:
https://www.instagram.com/the_dragon_and_rat_tale/?hl=en

Website:
https://donnabellebooks.wordpress.com/

https://depop.com/egirlismyasthetic

Printed in the United States
By Bookmasters